Funky Scales for Flute

COVERING GRADES 1–3 OF ALL THE MAJOR EXAMINATION BOARDS!

SIMON LESLEY

CHESTER MUSIC
(A division of Music Sales Limited)
8/9 Frith Street, London, W1D 3JB, England.

Exclusive distributors:
Chester Music
(A division of Music Sales Limited)
8/9 Frith Street, London W1D 3JB, England.

Order No. CH64625
ISBN 0-7119-9354-8
This book © Copyright 2002 by Chester Music.

Printed in the United Kingdom.
Cover designed by Chloë Alexander.
Music engraved by Note-orious Productions Limited.
Audio arranged by Note-orious Productions Limited.

Your Guarantee of Quality:
As publishers, we strive to produce every book to the highest commercial standards.
This book has been freshly engraved and carefully designed to minimise awkward page
turns making playing from it a real pleasure.
Particular care has been given to specifying acid-free, neutral-sized paper made from
pulps which have not been elemental chlorine bleached.
This pulp is from farmed sustainable forests and was produced with special regard for
the environment.
Throughout, the printing and binding have been planned to ensure a sturdy,
attractive publication which should give years of enjoyment.
If your copy fails to meet our high standards, please inform us and we will gladly
replace it or offer a refund.

Music Sales' complete catalogue describes thousands of titles and is available in full
colour sections by subject, direct from Music Sales Limited.
Please state your areas of interest and send a cheque/postal order for £1.50 for
postage to: Music Sales Limited, Newmarket Road, Bury St Edmunds, Suffolk IP33 3YB.

www.musicsales.com

C Major Scale
(no sharps or flats)

1 Octave

First try the basic 8-note scale:

1   2   3   4   5   6   7   8

A Twelfth

Then, if you can get the high notes, extend the same scale pattern into the next octave:

1 Octave In Rhythm (⊚ Tracks no.2 & 45)

Playing scales in a rhythm helps you to learn to control your scales:

Click on track: 1, 2, 3, 2, 2, 3

A Piece Using The Notes Of The Scale (⊚ Tracks no.3 & 46)

Most pieces are based on scales, and that is a good reason to learn them.
If you know which scale a piece is based on, you will find the piece much easier to play:

Click on track: 1, 2, 3, 4

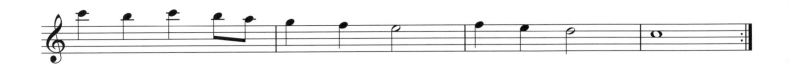

C Major Arpeggio
(no sharps or flats)

1 Octave

An arpeggio is made up of the 1st, 3rd and 5th notes of the scale.
Play this *triad*, followed by the top note of the octave:

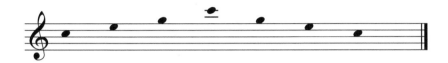

A Twelfth

A twelfth takes you as far as the 5th note of the next octave.
This means that you play up and down two *triads*.

triad = *group of three notes*

A Twelfth In Rhythm (Tracks no.4 & 47)

Click on track: 1, 2, 2, 2,

A Piece Based On The Arpeggio (Tracks no.5 & 48)

Click on track: 1, 2, 3, 4

G Major Scale
(1 sharp)

1 Octave

In order to have a major scale starting on G, you need to remember F#s.

(F#)   (F#)

2 Octaves

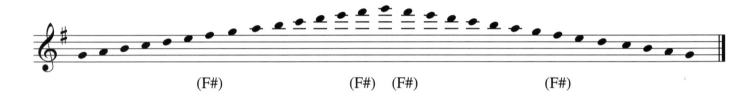

(F#)   (F#)   (F#)   (F#)

1 Octave In Rhythm (Tracks no.6 & 49)

You will need to know your ♯s and ♭s from memory, so no more reminders!

Click on track: 1, 2, 3, 2, 2, 3

A Piece Using The Notes Of The Scale (Tracks no.7 & 50)

Click on track: 1, 2, 3, 4

G Major Arpeggio
(1 sharp)

1 Octave

The note on which the scale starts and finishes is called the ***key-note***.

G   G   G

2 Octaves

G   G   G   G   G

2 Octaves In Rhythm (💿 Tracks no.8 & 51)

Click on track: 1, 2, 2, 2,

A Piece Based On The Arpeggio (💿 Tracks no.9 & 52)

Click on track: 1, 2, 3, 4

F Major Scale
(1 flat)

1 Octave

Try numbering the degrees of the scale in your head as you play.

1st 2nd 3rd 4th 5th 6th 7th 8th 7th 6th 5th 4th 3rd 2nd 1st

2 Octaves

Remember not to lose your place. Know where your *key-note* is.

F   F   F   F   F

1 Octave In Rhythm (Tracks no.10 & 53)

Click on track: 1, 2, 3, 2, 2, 3

A Piece Using The Notes Of The Scale (Tracks no.11 & 54)

Click on track: 1, 2, 3, 4

Did you notice that this was the same piece again, only it was based on a different scale?

F Major Arpeggio
(1 flat)

1 Octave

Notice that the 8th note is the same as the 1st. They are both the *key-note*.

     1st   3rd   5th   8th/1st   5th   3rd   1st

2 Octaves

Which is more helpful for you - numbering the degrees of the
scale, or remembering the *key-note*? You choose.

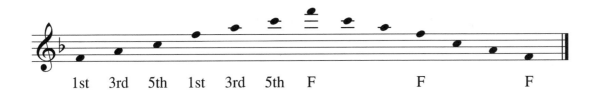

     1st   3rd   5th   1st   3rd   5th   F   F   F

2 Octaves In Rhythm (Tracks no.12 & 55)

Click on track: 1, 2, 2, 2,

A Piece Based On The Arpeggio (Tracks no.13 & 56)

Click on track: 1, 2, 3, 4

Did you notice that this was the same piece again, only it was based on a different scale?

D Major Scale
(2 sharps)

I Octave

2 Octaves

Think of the 2nd octave as a repeat of the 1st.

I Octave In Rhythm (Tracks no.14 & 57)

Click on track: 1, 2, 2, 2

A Piece Using The Notes Of The Scale (Tracks no.15 & 58)

This piece has a range of more than one octave.

Click on track: 1, 2, 3, 4

D Major Arpeggio
(2 sharps)

1 Octave

Arpeggios fit nicely into regular groups of three. Count '1', '2', '3' as you play.

2 Octaves

2 Octaves In Rhythm (💿 Tracks no.16 & 59)

Click on track: 1, 2, 3, 2, 2, 3

A Piece Based On The Arpeggio (💿 Tracks no.17 & 60)

This piece does not start on the *key-note*. Don't be confused!

Click on track: 1, 2, 3, 4

B♭ Major Scale
(2 flats)

I Octave

Don't forget to practise scales both tongued and slurred:

A Twelfth

I Octave In Rhythm (Tracks no.18 & 61)

This rhythm should be very snappy, especially if you are tonguing it.

Click on track: 1, 2, 2, 2

A Piece Using The Notes Of The Scale (Tracks no.19 & 62)

Do you know which degrees of the scale you are playing?
Think about them as you play:

Click on track: 1, 2, 3, 4

1st   5th (below)   2nd 3rd 4th   3rd   2nd   1st   4th 5th 6th   5th (etc.)

B♭ Major Arpeggio
(2 flats)

1 Octave

A Twelfth

A Twelfth In Rhythm (⊚ **Tracks no.20 & 63)**

Click on track: 1, 2, 3, 4, 5, 6

A Piece Based On The Arpeggio (⊚ **Tracks no.21 & 64)**

This piece is the same as the D major arpeggio piece. Really concentrate on following the shape of the melody:

Click on track: 1, 2, 3, 4

A Major Scale
(3 sharps)

1 Octave

A Twelfth

1 Octave In Rhythm (🔘 Tracks no.22 & 65)

Click on track: 1, 2, 2, 2

A Piece Using The Notes Of The Scale (🔘 Tracks no.23 & 66)

If you have been thinking about the degrees of the scale or following the shape of the melody,
you might like to try and finish off this piece yourself! (It is the same as the D major and B♭ major pieces)

Click on track: 1, 2, 3, 4

A Major Arpeggio
(3 sharps)

I Octave

A Twelfth

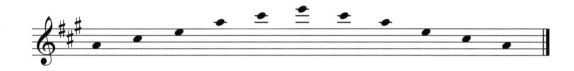

A Twelfth In Rhythm (Tracks no.24 & 67)

Click on track: 1, 2, 3, 4, 5, 6

A Piece Based On The Arpeggio (Tracks no.25 & 68)

Try finishing off this piece as well. What you are doing is called *transposition*,
which is moving the same tune into a different position, scale or key.
You can look at the B♭ major arpeggio page if it helps you to see the shape of the melody.

trans = across

Click on track: 1, 2, 3, 4

Major Scales

In order to play scales, it may help you to know a little about the theory behind them:

Major scales sound the way they do because of a set pattern of jumps between their notes. The distance between particular degrees of the scale is always the same, no matter which note the scale starts on. So, the scale always sounds the same, too.

For every major scale, here is the pattern of jumps from one note to the next, starting on the **key-note** (the distances are measured in half-steps - e.g. C ➤ C♯ is a **half-step**):

	+2		+2		+1		+2		+2		+2		+1	
Key-note	→	2nd	→	3rd	→	4th	→	5th	→	6th	→	7th	→	8th

Using the piano keyboard below to help measure the number of half-steps, try and work out the missing note names from these major scales (**half-step = +1**):

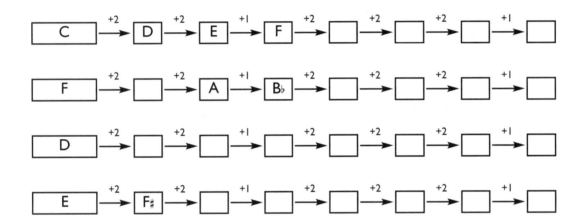

A Helpful Hint:

The letters have to go in alphabetical order, but you need to know about the number of half steps in order to get the ♯ or ♭ correct.

Another Helpful Hint:

At the 8th note, you should arrive at the **key-note** again!

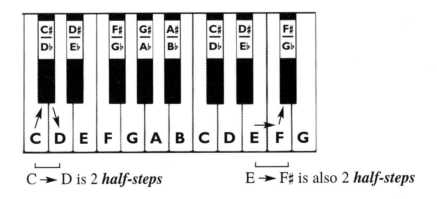

C ➤ D is 2 **half-steps**   E ➤ F♯ is also 2 **half-steps**

Another word for **half-step** is a **semi-tone**. Two **half-steps** make a whole step, or **tone**.

Minor Scales

A Tale Of Two Brothers!

Every minor scale is related to a major scale. You may like to think of every minor scale as having a big brother or *relative major*. Therefore, every minor scale must have a little brother or *relative minor*. Any two brothers, major and minor, are brothers because they share the same key signature (that being the number of ♯s or ♭s for that scale). For example, both C major and its *relative minor* brother have no ♯s or ♭s.

Relative minor brothers are easy to find, because they always live 3 *half-steps* <u>down</u> from their bigger, *relative major* brother. So to find the name of C major's *relative minor* brother, for example, you must travel <u>down</u> 3 *half-steps*:

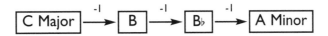

Try finding the *relative minors* of these major scales:

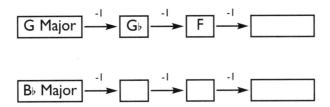

Brotherly Arguments!

Unfortunately minor scales are awkward, and do not agree with their major brothers about the sharing of a key signature. They have their own additional sharps, which do not appear in the key signature but are added as you play through the minor scale. There are also two different versions of minor scales - *harmonic* and *melodic*.

Harmonic minors sharpen their 7th note. For example, A minor *harmonic*, with no ♯s or ♭s in its key signature, goes as follows:

A, B, C, D, E, F, G♯, A

Melodic minors are more awkward still, sharpening their 6th and 7th notes on the way up only, then cancelling them again on the way down. For example, A minor *melodic* goes as follows:

up: A, B, C, D, E, F♯, G♯, A   down: A, G♮, F♮, E, D, C, B, A

Harmonic minors are based around the idea of *harmony* - chords, bass lines, etc.

Melodic minors are based around the idea of *melody*, which flows freely, pushing upwards and falling downwards.

Try and use the information on these two pages to help you remember your scale patterns.

A Minor Scale

(relative minor of C major = no sharps or flats)

Harmonic, 1 Octave

For *harmonic* minors, remember to sharpen the 7th note, even though...
...it does not appear in the key signature!

A Twelfth

Melodic, 1 Octave

For *melodic* minors, remember to sharpen the 6th and 7th note on the way up only.
Cancel them again on the way down.

A Twelfth

A Piece Using The Notes Of The Scale (Tracks no.26 & 69)

This piece uses the *harmonic* minor to make up its melody.

Click on track: 1, 2, 3, 4

A Minor Arpeggio
(relative minor of C major = no sharps or flats)

1 Octave

Because arpeggios are made up of only the 1st, 3rd and 5th notes of the scale, there is no difference between *harmonic* and *melodic*.

A Twelfth

A Twelfth In Rhythm ( Tracks no.27 & 70)

Click on track: 1, 2, 2, 2,

A Piece Based On The Arpeggio ( Tracks no.28 & 71)

You don't have to worry about sharpening 6ths or 7ths when playing minor arpeggios!

Click on track: 1, 2, 3, 4

E Minor Scale

(relative minor of G major = 1 sharp)

Harmonic, 1 Octave

You will need to remember the F♯ in the key signature as well as the sharpened 7th note.

2 Octaves

Melodic, 1 Octave

If you know the relative major scale well, it may help you with remembering the pattern for the minor scale.
In this case, imagine you are playing G major, except starting on E.
Apart from the extra sharps on the way up, this scale is exactly that - a G major scale starting on an E.

2 Octaves

A Piece Using The Notes Of The Scale (◎ Tracks no.29 & 72)

Click on track: 1, 2, 3, 4

E Minor Arpeggio
(relative minor of G major = 1 sharp)

1 Octave

2 Octaves

2 Octaves In Rhythm (◎ Tracks no.30 & 73)

Click on track: 1, 2, 3, 4, 5, 6

A Piece Based On The Arpeggio (◎ Tracks no.31 & 74)

Click on track: 1, 2, 3, 4

D Minor Scale

(relative minor of F major = 1 flat)

Harmonic, 1 Octave

If you find counting to seven tricky, you can think of the 7th note as the one before the octave.

2 Octaves

Melodic, 1 Octave

For this scale, notice how sharpening the 6th note means sharpening the B♭ from the key signature.
So, if you sharpen a flat (♭), you get a natural (♮). You still need to cancel this on the way down.

2 Octaves

A Piece Using The Notes Of The Scale (💿 Tracks no.32 & 75)

Click on track: 1, 2, 3, 4

Did you notice that this was the same piece again?
Could you have worked out the melody by transposing from the A or E minor pieces?

D Minor Arpeggio
(relative minor of F major = 1 flat)

1 Octave

2 Octaves

2 Octaves In Rhythm (Tracks no.33 & 76)

Click on track: 1, 2, 3, 4, 5, 6

A Piece Based On The Arpeggio (Tracks no.34 & 77)

Click on track: 1, 2, 3, 4

Did you notice that this was the same piece again?
Could you have worked out the melody by transposing from the A or E minor pieces?

B Minor Scale
(relative minor of D major = 2 sharps)

Harmonic, 1 Octave

Don't start to panic about all these sharps!
It may help to think about the *relative major* as you play (D major, in this instance).

A Twelfth

Melodic, 1 Octave

Think: D major scale starting on B

A Twelfth

A Piece Using The Notes Of The Melodic Scale (⊚ Tracks no.35 & 78)

Notice how the melody has sharpened 6ths and 7ths when it is rising, but normal ones when it is falling.

Click on track: 1, 2, 3, 4

24

B Minor Arpeggio
(relative minor of D major = 2 sharps)

1 Octave

A Twelfth

A Twelfth In Rhythm (Tracks no.36 & 79)

Click on track: 1, 2, 2, 2

A Piece Based On The Scale And Arpeggio (Tracks no.37 & 80)

This piece uses a mixture of arpeggio and scale patterns.

Click on track: 1, 2, 3, 4

G Minor Scale

(relative minor of B♭ major = 2 flats)

Harmonic, 1 Octave

Remember to play both tongued and slurred.

2 Octaves

Melodic, 1 Octave

Keep your playing extremely under control, each note being the same volume and speed.

2 Octaves

A Piece Using The Notes Of The Melodic Scale (Tracks no.38 & 81)

Click on track: 1, 2, 3, 4

G Minor Arpeggio
(relative minor of B♭ major = 2 flats)

1 Octave

2 Octaves

2 Octaves In Rhythm (Tracks no.39 & 82)

Click on track: 1, 2, 3, 4, 5, 6

A Piece Based On The Scale And Arpeggio (Tracks no.40 & 83)

Try mixing your articulation, tonguing and slurring in the same piece.

Click on track: 1, 2, 3, 4

F# Minor Scale

(relative minor of A major = 3 sharps)

Harmonic, I Octave

E# is the same note as F♮. The name E# is used because the note names of a scale must go in alphabetical order. It would <u>not</u> be correct to call them F#, G#, A, B, C#, D, **F**, F#. The notes should be F#, G#, A, B, C#, D, **E#**, F#.

2 Octaves

Melodic, I Octave

2 Octaves

A Piece Using The Notes Of The Melodic Scale (⊚ Tracks no.41 & 84)

Click on track: 1, 2, 3, 4

F♯ Minor Arpeggio
(relative minor of A major = 3 sharps)

1 Octave

Remember to count '1', '2', '3' when playing arpeggios.

2 Octaves

2 Octaves In Rhythm ( Tracks no.42 & 85)

Click on track: 1, 2, 3, 4, 5, 6

A Piece Based On The Scale And Arpeggio (Tracks no.43 & 86)

Click on track: 1, 2, 3, 4

For a real challenge, you could try working out this melody by looking at the B minor page and transposing it!

Transposing From Scale To Scale
Major Keys

Here is a small melody in C major. Try transposing it into different keys.
Remember to think about degrees of the scale, where the *key-note* is, and to follow the shape of the melody.

C major

1st   2nd   3rd   5th   etc.

G major

1st   2nd   3rd   5th   etc.

F major

1st   2nd   3rd   5th   etc.

D major

B♭ major

A major

Transposing From Scale To Scale
Minor Keys

Here is a small melody in A minor (harmonic). Try transposing it into different keys.
Remember to think about degrees of the scale, where the *key-note* is, and to follow the shape of the melody.

A minor

8th   7th 6th 5th   6th   etc.

E minor

8th   7th 6th 5th   6th   etc.

D minor

8th   7th 6th 5th   6th   etc.

B minor

G minor

F# minor

Chromatic Scales

Chromatic scales are not quite the same as majors and minors. *Chromatic* comes from the Greek word 'chromata' meaning 'decorations', and so *chromatic* scales travel by the smallest jumps possible - by *half-steps*.

This means that you play all the black and white notes, every sharp (♯), flat (♭) and natural (♮).

It also means that it doesn't matter where you start - every pattern is the same!
Because you play every note, there are no key signatures and a *chromatic* scale could happen in the middle of any piece.

1 Octave Starting on F

1 Octave Starting on G

1 Octave Starting on F In Rhythm

There is one rhythm which suits *chromatic* scales extremely well.
Play them in groups of 4, with a little accent on the beginning of each group.

A Piece Based On A Chromatic Scale (◎ Tracks no.44 & 87)

Click on track: 1, 2, 3, 4